9733    3488ⅷ081988
Smo  Smolinski, Diane

**AUTHOR**

Important People

**TITLE**

of the Revolutionary War

| DATE DUE | BORROWER'S NAME | ROOM NUMBER |
|---|---|---|
| C3/20/0? | Hector Anaya | |
| 2-5-03 | Kobe Jones | 208 |
| | Carlos | |
| 9/9/09 | Daniel | 207 |
| | | |

# Important People
## of the
# Revolutionary War

**Diane Smolinski**

**Series Consultant:
Lieutenant Colonel G.A. LoFaro**

Heinemann Library
Chicago, Illinois

Designed by Herman Adler Design
Printed in Hong Kong

06 05 04 03 02
10 9 8 7 6 5 4 3 2 1

**Library of Congress Cataloging-in-Publication Data**

Smolinski, Diane, 1950-
    Important People of the Revolutionary War /
Diane Smolinski.
        p. cm. -- (Americans at War: The Revolutionary War)
Includes bibliographical references and index.
    ISBN 1-58810-278-5 (lib. bdg.)
    ISBN 1-58810-559-8 (pbk. bdg.)
    1. United States--History--Revolution, 1775-1783--
Biography--Juvenile literature. [1. United States--
History--Revolution, 1775-1783--Biography.]  I. Title.
    E206 .S66 2001
    973.3'092'2--dc21

                            2001001617

**Acknowledgments**
The author and publishers are grateful to the
following for permission to reproduce copyright
material: p. 4 (clockwise from top right) Bettmann/
Corbis, Corbis, The Granger Collection, New York,
Corbis; p. 5, 25 Peter Newark's Military Pictures;
p. 6, 8, 23, 24, 27, 28 Bettmann/Corbis; p. 7, 9, 11,
12 Corbis; p. 10, 13, 14, 16, 20, 29 top North Wind
Picture Archives; p. 15, 26 Archivo Iconografico,
S.A./Corbis; p. 17, 18, 19, 21, 29 bottom The Granger
Collection, New York; p. 22 Clements Library,
University of Michigan.

Cover photograph © The Granger Collection,
New York

Every effort has been made to contact copyright
holders of any material reproduced in this book. Any
omissions will be rectified in subsequent printings if
notice is given to the publisher.

**About the Author**
Diane Smolinski is a teacher for the Seminole
County School District in Florida. She earned B.S.
of Education degrees from Duquesne University and
Slippery Rock University in Pennsylvania. For the past
fourteen years, Diane has taught the Revolutionary
War curriculum to fourth and fifth graders. Diane
has previously authored a series of Civil War books
for young readers. She lives with her husband, two
daughters, and their cat, Pepper.

**About the Consultant**
G.A. LoFaro is a lieutenant colonel in the U.S. Army
currently stationed at Fort McPherson, Georgia. After
graduating from West Point, he was commissioned in
the infantry. He has served in a variety of positions
in the 82nd Airborne Division, the Ranger Training
Brigade, and Second Infantry Division in Korea.
He has a Masters Degree in U.S. History from the
University of Michigan and is completing his Ph.D
in U.S. History at the State University of New York
at Stony Brook. He has also served six years on the
West Point faculty where he taught military history
to cadets.

Some words are shown in bold, **like this.**
You can find out what they mean by looking in the glossary.

# Contents

# Many Build a Nation

**The individuals featured in this book were among the many people who made important contributions to the Revolutionary War. To get a more complete picture of this war, it is important to look at the men and women who were loyal to the British cause as well as people who fought for the American cause.**

Military leaders, soldiers, political **statesmen,** spies, women, Native Americans, and slaves were all involved in the struggle for freedom that was called the Revolutionary War. Citizens who fought bravely for the **colonies** were called **Patriots.** Those who fought just as bravely for the British were called **Loyalists.**

*Joseph Brant—Native American Loyalist*

*Nathanael Greene— Patriot and Soldier*

*Lydia Darragh—Patriot Spy*

*General Charles Cornwallis—British Leader*

4

## Town Crier News

- Female **camp followers** did not get paid, but received food for themselves and for their children.

- Many slaves who joined the military were promised freedom when the war was over.

Colonists supported the soldiers in both armies in many different ways. Political statesmen used their abilities to read, write, and speak to convince others to support their cause. Women could not officially join the military as soldiers, so many followed the armies. They did chores for the soldiers, many of whom were their husbands. The military depended on men and women who lived in the communities to provide them with information about the opposing side. Slaves fought beside free men. Native Americans sometimes served as scouts and guides for the armies.

Even though many people made contributions as individuals, the outcome of the Revolutionary War was determined by the combined efforts of all of these different groups.

*Colonial troops marched against the British to the sound of drums and **fifes**.*

# George Washington (1732–1799)

**George Washington's leadership and military skills were important to the success of the Continental Army. He played a large part in defeating the British.**

## Early Years

George Washington's ancestors traveled from England to settle in the North American **colonies.** George was born in Westmoreland County, Virginia. He wanted to join the British Royal Navy, but instead learned how to work as a surveyor, measuring land. At age twenty, Washington **inherited** some land. He became a wealthy Virginia planter and businessman.

## Political Career

Washington served for sixteen years in the Virginia House of Burgesses, which was the first group of people elected to make laws in colonial America. He was a justice of the peace and a representative for Virginia to the first and second **Continental Congresses.** In 1789, George Washington was elected the first president of the United States. He served two terms, but turned down the opportunity to serve a third term.

## Military Career

Washington joined the Virginia **militia** in 1753. He gained valuable military experience fighting for the British in the **French and Indian War.** In 1758, he **resigned** from the military and returned home to his Virginia plantation, Mount Vernon.

### Town Crier News

- When elected president, George Washington moved to New York City, the capital of the United States at this time.

- The national capital city of Washington, D.C., is named after our first president. Washington chose this site for a permanent capital city. It was originally called Federal City.

*George Washington learned to survey land at the age of sixteen.*

*General George Washington took command of the Continental Army.*

In 1774, Washington again joined the Virginia militia in support of the **rebellion** against Great Britain. During the Revolutionary War, Washington served as the commander in chief of the Continental Army. He worked hard to convince the soldiers to keep fighting. He also worked hard to convince political leaders to provide his soldiers with food, clothing, and enough pay so that they could stay healthy and would continue fighting. Washington officially resigned from the army on December 23, 1783, after the colonists had won their independence. He returned home to Mount Vernon, Virginia.

## Town Crier News

When George Washington died in 1799, he left instructions that the 300 slaves working on his plantation were to be freed. Half were to be freed upon his death, and the other half were to be freed upon his wife Martha's death. Martha freed most of them prior to her death in 1802.

# General Thomas Gage

**(1721–1787)**

**Thomas Gage was born and educated in England. He was a professional soldier in the British Army—being in the military was his chosen career. Gage came to North America to serve in the French and Indian War, which was fought in the American colonies from 1754 to 1763.**

General Gage later became the first commander in chief of the British forces in the colonies. In 1774, he was appointed the governor of Massachusetts. The following year, he sent troops to Concord to destroy weapons and ammunition belonging to colonists. British troops exchanged musket fire with local **militiamen.** This was the start of the Revolutionary War. Later that same year, General Gage commanded the British Army at the Battle of Bunker Hill, near Boston.

Although the British won the Battle of Bunker Hill, Gage was ordered to return to England. Government officials were unhappy with Gage for not stopping the **rebellion** in the colonies.

## Town Crier News

As commander in chief, General Thomas Gage planned, directed, and gave orders for the British attack on Bunker Hill, but he did not actually fight in the battle. Instead, he sent General Sir William Howe and other military commanders to carry out his orders on the battlefield.

# General Sir William Howe (1729–1814)

**Like General Thomas Gage, General Sir William Howe was a professional soldier in the British Army. He, too, first served in North America during the French and Indian War. Howe and other British military commanders brought leadership and experience to the battlefield during the Revolutionary War.**

When General Gage returned to England, Howe became the commander in chief of all British forces in North America. Before Gage left, Howe led troops to Boston to help fight the Battle of Bunker Hill. He also fought in the battles of Long Island, White Plains, Brandywine, and Germantown.

Even though his troops won many battles, British officials were upset that General Howe failed to win the war. In 1777, he **resigned** from his position as commander in chief and returned to England. There, he continued to serve in the British Army and became involved in politics.

## Town Crier News

- Sir William Howe was a member of British **Parliament** from 1758 to 1780.

- Howe tried to win battles with the fewest victims possible.

- Howe was criticized for being too easy on the rebellious **Patriots.**

- His brother, Richard Howe, was also involved in the Revolutionary War.

# Ethan Allen (1738–1789)

In 1757, Ethan Allen helped to defend Fort William Henry during the **French and Indian War.** After this war, he made kettles, metal pots, as a profession. In 1769, he moved to the area that is now called Vermont. There, he became Colonel Commandant of the Green Mountain Boys. This group was formed to keep New Yorkers from settling on land in this area.

During the Revolutionary War, Ethan Allen led a group that took Fort Ticonderoga in New York from the British. Next, Allen tried unsuccessfully to capture Montreal, Canada. Allen was captured and sent to England. Upon his return to the **colonies,** Allen was given the rank of lieutenant colonel for his courage and loyalty.

## Town Crier News

- The Green Mountain Boys were originally a group of men that protected settlers west of the Green Mountains from people from New York who wanted this land.

- George III, the King of England, had declared that the land belonged to New York.

*The Green Mountain Boys did not want settlers from New York to move into their land and use their resources, so they stole New Yorkers' cattle and burned their cabins.*

# Nathanael Greene (1742–1786)

**Nathanael Greene was a private in the Rhode Island militia and later a major general in the Continental Army. He first fought in many battles in the northern colonies. Then, in 1780, Greene took command of the Continental Army in the South.**

General Greene was able to keep the commander of the British Army, General Cornwallis, from capturing North Carolina. He then led his army into South Carolina, where he attacked British outposts. Greene played an important role in the southern battles that helped to determine the outcome of the war.

Greene's Continental forces eventually forced the British Army to retreat to Wilmington, North Carolina, and then to Yorktown, Virginia. At Yorktown, General Cornwallis surrendered his army in what was the last major battle of the Revolutionary War.

## Town Crier News

- Before the Revolutionary War, Greene was an ironworker and a merchant.

- In June 1775, he became the youngest general serving in the Continental Army. He was 32 years old.

- Greene served several terms in the Rhode Island legislature.

- Greene spent his later life in Georgia. He died at age 43.

# General Lord Charles Cornwallis (1738–1805)

**In 1776, Lord Charles Cornwallis volunteered to come to the North American colonies from England. At the beginning of the Revolutionary War, he fought in many battles in the northern colonies.**

In 1780, Cornwallis sailed to South Carolina with another British Army leader, Sir Henry Clinton, to help the **Loyalists** return the southern colonies to British rule. After the **Patriots** were defeated at Charleston, South Carolina, Clinton returned to New York. Cornwallis became the commander of the British Army in the southern colonies. He was successful in many battles in the South, but lost many of his soldiers. In the end, Continental and French forces trapped his British forces at Yorktown, Virginia. Cornwallis had to surrender. This was the last major battle of the Revolutionary War.

## Town Crier News

- Cornwallis purchased his **commission** in the British Army in 1756. That was an acceptable way to become an officer at the time.

- Cornwallis was most successful fighting the Continental Army in open-field battles. He had a harder time leading his troops against Continental riflemen in woodland battles and responding to surprise attacks.

- On the day that Cornwallis surrendered at Yorktown, Sir Henry Clinton was sailing from New York City with troops and supplies to help him.

## Service Outside the Colonies

Cornwallis joined the British Army in 1756. He served in Germany during the European conflict called the Seven Years' War, which was fought from 1756 to 1763. In the North American colonies, this same war was being fought as the **French and Indian War.**

Cornwallis also served in public office for the British government in the North American colonies. He gained valuable experience as a leader of British forces during the Revolutionary War. This leadership experience earned him the respect of the British **Parliament.**

*In 1786, Cornwallis was made the governor-general of the British colony of India. Later, he served as **viceroy** of Ireland.*

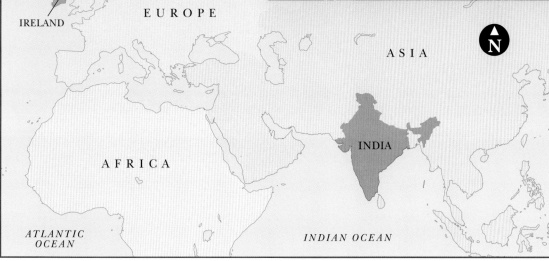

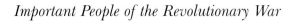

# French Allies

It was common for European nations to hire soldiers from other countries to help them fight wars. The British hired soldiers to help them fight the American Revolutionary War. In the 1770s, the American **colonists** did not have enough money to hire soldiers from other countries. The newly formed colonial navy was also no match for the powerful British Navy.

Statesmen such as Benjamin Franklin went to Europe to speak with leaders from other countries to ask for help. France sent troops, money, and the help of their strong navy. These French soldiers and sailors helped the colonists win the war.

## Town Crier News

In a **document** called The Treaty of Alliance, France agreed to help the colonial soldiers fight the British in the American Revolutionary War.

*Franklin spoke to the court of Louis XVI of France and explained the colonists' need for support.*

# Marquis de Lafayette

**(1757–1834)**

**Before the American Revolution began, the Marquis de Lafayette served in the French Army. He used his influence and wealth to convince the French government to give aid to the colonies. Lafayette bought a ship with part of his fortune and sailed to the North American colonies with other French military officers in 1777.**

After Lafayette fought in the Battle of Brandywine, Congress appointed him a **major general** in the Continental Army. He would not accept payment for his services. Lafayette spent the winter of 1777 to 1778 with the Continental Army at Valley Forge, Pennsylvania, and became a close friend of George Washington. Lafayette helped convince the French king to send soldiers to help the colonists. Lafayette's troops helped trap Cornwallis's army at Yorktown, Virginia, in 1781. After the British surrendered, Lafayette returned to Paris, France.

## Town Crier News

- Lafayette's full name was Marie Joseph Paul Yves Roch Gilbert du Motier.

- His title was the Marquis de Lafayette. A marquis is a French nobleman.

- Even after the Revolutionary War, Lafayette continued to urge the French to support the United States.

# Deborah Sampson (1760–1827)

**During the Revolutionary War, women were not allowed to join the army. Deborah Sampson disguised herself as a man in order to join the Continental Army.**

### Early Years

Deborah's parents owned a small farm in Massachusetts. After her father left, her mother could not care for the farm and all the children. Deborah was sent to live with relatives. Later, Deborah worked as an **indentured servant** for the Benjamin Thomas family. She helped with housework and farm work. On some days, Deborah was allowed to attend school.

In 1779, Deborah's contract as an indentured servant with the Thomas household ended. To earn a living, she taught school and did some spinning and weaving.

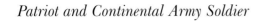

### A Continental Soldier

In 1782, Deborah enlisted in the Continental Army for three years in the Fourth Massachusetts Regiment under the name of Robert Shurtleff. That was the name of Deborah's brother who had died. Deborah was wounded twice, but she was able to keep her secret. She then caught a fever and had to be taken to a hospital. The doctor soon realized that Deborah was a woman.

Once she was well, the doctor wrote a letter for Deborah to deliver to her commander. Deborah's commander was surprised, but not disappointed with her. She had fought and earned the respect of her fellow soldiers on the battlefield. Deborah was honorably **discharged** in 1783.

*Deborah Sampson, shown here presenting a letter to General Washington from her commanding officer, was one of the first female lecturers in the country.*

## After the War

Deborah returned to Massachusetts and married Benjamin Gannett, a farmer. They had three children. Deborah toured towns and told her story.

## Town Crier News

- In 1792, after many years of asking, the Commonwealth of Massachusetts and the government finally paid Deborah money she was owed during the war. The government paid her four dollars per month.

- A group of people in Congress awarded Deborah's husband a pension after her death and wrote:

    *The whole of the American Revolution records no case like this, and furnishes no other similar example of female heroism, fidelity, and courage...*

# Lydia Darragh (1729–1789)

**Lydia Darragh came from Dublin, Ireland, to live in Philadelphia, in the North American colony of Pennsylvania. Women were not permitted to join the army at this time, so Darragh found another way to help. She became a spy.**

In 1777, the British controlled the city of Philadelphia. Lydia Darragh lived across the street from the British Headquarters. British officers sometimes held meetings in the Darragh house. Darragh heard the officers planning an attack on the Patriots at Whitemarsh, the place where General Washington's Continental Army was camped.

No one was allowed to leave Philadelphia at this time without the permission of the British, so Darragh received a pass to visit a nearby mill to obtain flour. While she was out of the city, she passed a message to General Washington that told him of the planned attack. The British were unsuccessful in this attack.

## Town Crier News

- Darragh's oldest son was in the Continental Army.

- Lydia Darragh and her family were Quakers. Quakers, also called Friends, generally stayed out of the war. Thinking that the Darraghs would not take sides in the war, the British felt that their home was a safe place to hold their meetings.

- When the war was over, Darragh went back to her normal life.

*Lydia Darragh tells one of General Washington's aides about the British Army's plans to attack the Continental Army at Whitemarsh, near Philadelphia, on December 4, 1777.*

# James Armistead (1760–1832)

James Armistead was a slave. As a slave, he had to get permission from his owner to join the army. In 1781, his commanding officer was the Marquis de Lafayette. Lafayette asked Armistead to go into a British Army camp and pretend he wanted to help the British Army. Armistead became a servant to Benedict Arnold and then to General Cornwallis. He sent back information about British troops to the Continental Army.

After awhile, General Cornwallis asked Armistead to spy on Lafayette and the Continental Army. Armistead remained loyal to the **Patriots.** He gave false information to the British while continuing to give correct information to the Patriots.

## Town Crier News

- After the war, Armistead added Lafayette to his name in honor of the Revolutionary War leader, making him James Armistead Lafayette.

- In 1786, Armistead received his freedom from being a slave.

# Benedict Arnold (1741–1801)

**Benedict Arnold was a Patriot military leader at the beginning of the Revolutionary War. Later in the war, he became a traitor by spying for the British and serving in the British Army.**

## Continental Soldier

Arnold was a leader in the Connecticut **militia** before joining the Continental Army. He fought many successful battles for the Patriots. He forced the surrender of Fort Ticonderoga in 1775, blocked Guy Carlton's advance at the Battle of Valcour Island in 1776, and helped the Patriots defeat the British at Saratoga, New York, in 1777. Arnold became unhappy that he was not being advanced quickly enough. George Washington tried to make him happy by making him the military commander of Philadelphia when the British left. But Arnold argued with a lot of people, and this made him many enemies. When he was blamed for doing something wrong, he became angry and **resigned** his command.

## British Spy

Arnold was very angry, and wanted to do something to hurt the colonists, so he decided to become a spy for the British. General Washington did not know of Arnold's decision, and appointed him commander of **West Point** in New York. Arnold planned to hand over this military post to the British.

*In their meeting on September 21, 1780, Arnold gave British Major André important information about West Point. Arnold told André to hide the information in his boot.*

John André, a major in the British Army, was captured with papers describing this plan. The papers told of Benedict Arnold's part in the plans.

Leaving his family behind, Arnold escaped to the Hudson River where a British warship was waiting. It took him to British-held New York City. The British made Arnold a general. He fought as a **Loyalist** for the rest of the war.

Once the war ended, Arnold and his family sailed to England with many other Loyalists. He lived the rest of his life in London, England, as a merchant.

## Town Crier News

- Before becoming a soldier, Arnold was a successful merchant in New Haven, Connecticut.

- Arnold had five children. His four sons became British military officers, and his daughter married one.

- It was later proven that Arnold's wife Margaret had taken part in the West Point plot, too.

# Ann Bates (1748–1801)

**Ann Bates and her husband stayed loyal to the British when the war began. She helped the British by spying for them.**

During the Revolutionary War, Bates pretended to be a traveling saleswoman who sold items such as thread and cooking pots to **camp followers** of the Continental Army. However, as she sold items in the camps, she gathered information about Continental Army troops.

After the war, Bates went to England with many other **Loyalists.** She lived in poverty in England and was very angry toward the British government. Since Bates had helped the British so much during the Revolutionary War, she felt they should have provided her with money to live a better life.

## Town Crier News

- Before the Revolutionary War, Ann Bates was a teacher in Philadelphia, Pennsylvania.

- Bates was very knowledgeable about specific types of weapons she saw while spying for the British because her husband was a gun repairman for the British Army.

*This is a letter written by Ann Bates, in which she explains that an unnamed woman has come to town. This woman is another spy. Bates explains that this woman will go talk with a man in order to get information from him. Like Bates often did, this woman will act like she is merely a traveling saleswoman. The woman will not return to town until she has gathered useful information.*

# Benjamin Franklin (1706–1790)

*"There never was a good war or a bad peace."*
**—Benjamin Franklin, in a letter to Josiah Quincy, 1783**

Benjamin Franklin was 69 years old by the time the Revolutionary War broke out in the **colonies.** He was not a soldier, but his speaking and writing skills enabled him to help the colonies gain independence from Great Britain.

## Early Years

Benjamin Franklin was born in Boston, Massachusetts, in 1706. He had sixteen brothers and sisters. Franklin went to school until he was about ten years old. He then worked with his father, who was a soap and candle maker. When Franklin was twelve years old, he became an **apprentice** for his brother James, who was a printer. Franklin had a curious mind and was interested in many things. He read many books and became an educated man.

*One of Franklin's first jobs as a printer was to print the paper money used at that time in Pennsylvania. This money looked very different from the money we use today.*

## Successful Printer and Publisher

In 1724, Franklin went to England on a business trip. Business did not work out as he had planned. He worked as a printer's helper for a time in England and then returned to the **colonies** in 1726. Franklin settled in Philadelphia and became the new owner of a newspaper called the *Pennsylvania Gazette*.

n 1732 he published the first *Poor Richard's Almanack*. An almanac is a book that is published once a year. It is arranged like a calendar and contains many facts about many different subjects. Facts about the weather, times of the daily sunrises and sunsets, and other pieces of information were included. Franklin also wrote thoughtful poems and sayings in his almanacs. His almanac became very popular with the colonists.

### Town Crier News

- In addition to interesting facts, *Poor Richard's Almanack* contained a number of wise sayings:

  "Haste makes waste."
  "Lost time is never found again."
  "A true friend is the best Possession."

- While living in the city of Philadelphia, Pennsylvania, Franklin established the first library at which the public was allowed to check out books.

*Benjamin Franklin published* Poor Richard's Almanack *from 1732 to 1757. He used the name Richard Saunders as the publisher instead of his real name. He sold about 10,000 copies each year, a large amount for this time period.*

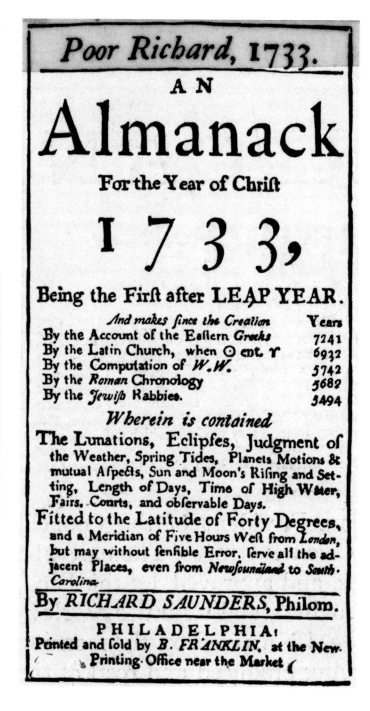

Poor Richard, 1733.

AN

Almanack

For the Year of Chrift

1733,

Being the Firft after LEAP YEAR.

| *And makes fince the Creation* | **Years** |
|---|---|
| By the Account of the Eaftern *Greeks* | 7241 |
| By the Latin Church, when ☉ ent. ♈ | 6932 |
| By the Computation of *W.W.* | 5742 |
| By the *Roman* Chronology | 5682 |
| By the *Jewifh* Rabbies. | 5494 |

*Wherein is contained*

The Lunations, Eclipfes, Judgment of the Weather, Spring Tides, Planets Motions & mutual Afpects, Sun and Moon's Rifing and Setting, Length of Days, Time of High Water, Fairs, Courts, and obfervable Days.

Fitted to the Latitude of Forty Degrees, and a Meridian of Five Hours Weft from *London*, but may without fenfible Error, ferve all the adjacent Places, even from *Newfoundland* to *South Carolina*.

By RICHARD SAUNDERS, Philom.

PHILADELPHIA:

Printed and fold by *B. FRANKLIN*, at the New Printing-Office near the Market.

## Political Service to His Nation

Benjamin Franklin had a long career as a political **statesman** in the American colonies. He served in the Pennsylvania Assembly from 1750 to 1764. In 1753, he became deputy postmaster general, where he was in charge of all the mail in the northern colonies. In 1764, he went to England for eleven years as a spokesman for the colonies.

On his return to the colonies in 1775, he represented Pennsylvania in the Second **Continental Congress.** He was also a member of a committee chosen to write the Declaration of Independence. Franklin later traveled to France to get financial and military assistance and help **negotiate** the peace treaty to end the Revolutionary War.

After the war, Franklin remained active in politics. He returned from Paris to Philadelphia and helped write the U.S. Constitution in 1787.

### Town Crier News

- Franklin was very talented in the field of science as well as in writing and politics.

- He is credited with many inventions, including bifocal glasses, good for seeing both near and far, and the lightning rod. He also experimented with electricity and invented the Franklin Stove.

- Franklin received a medal in 1753 for his successful experiments with electricity.

*During the Revolutionary War, Franklin's talents as a statesman made him very important to the Patriot cause.*

# King George III (1738–1820)

In 1760, at the age of 22, George III was crowned the king of England. As king, George III had a great deal of power. He approved many policies that created **discontent** among the citizens in the **colonies**. The colonists complained to him that his laws were unfair, but he refused to listen.

These complaints led to **rebellion** in the North American colonies, and war broke out. Even when British leaders wanted to end the war, George III wanted to keep fighting.

George III is believed to have had a disease that eventually caused him to become incapable of making decisions. His oldest son took care of his political duties during the last nine years of his reign.

*The king's full name was George William Frederick. He had fifteen children. He is said to have been a good husband and father.*

## Town Crier News

The Declaration of Independence charges King George III with 27 misuses of power. Some of these abuses were the following:

• *He has kept among us, in Times of Peace, Standing Armies, without the consent of our Legislatures.*

• *cutting off our Trade with all Parts of the World*

• *imposing Taxes on us without our Consent*

• *He has plundered our Seas, ravaged our Coasts, burnt our Towns, and destroyed the Lives of our People.*

# Paul Revere (1735–1818)

*"Listen, my children, and you shall hear*
*Of the midnight ride of Paul Revere*
*On the eighteenth of April, in Seventy-five..."*
**—from "Paul Revere's Ride" by Henry Wadsworth Longfellow**

On the evening of April 18, 1775, British troops left Boston, Massachusetts, and headed toward the town of Concord. Paul Revere and William Dawes also left Boston—to warn colonists in Lexington and Concord that the British were coming. Both Revere and Dawes were captured before reaching Concord, but the British did not find the weapons or the **Patriot** leaders they had set out to find.

Revere was just one of many colonists who believed deeply in the cause to gain freedom from British rule. Born in Boston, Massachusetts, in 1735, Paul Revere became a silversmith and **engraver.** He fought in the **French and Indian War,** which was fought in the American colonies from 1754 to 1763. Throughout the Revolutionary War, Revere supported the Patriots. After the war, Revere returned to work as a silversmith and engraver.

## Town Crier News

In 1773, many colonists were unhappy with British taxes on the sale of tea. So, on December 16, 1773, colonists dressed as Native Americans, climbed aboard British merchant ships, and tossed tea the ships were carrying into the Boston Harbor. Paul Revere helped plan this event, known as the Boston Tea Party. The Revolutionary War began soon afterwards.

# Joseph Brant (1742–1807)

**During the Revolutionary War, both armies welcomed the support of the Native Americans. Most Native American tribes expected the British to win the war and sided with them. They hoped that supporting the British would keep settlers from moving west onto Native American land.**

Joseph Brant was a Mohawk Iroquois Chief. As a young man, he had fought with the British in the **French and Indian War.** During the Revolutionary War, Brant convinced many Mohawks and other Native Americans to support the British. He also led raids on **Patriot** settlers, in an effort to keep them from taking more land from the Mohawks.

After the war, Brant tried to **negotiate** a land settlement for the Native Americans with the new American government, but no agreement could be reached. Brant received land in Canada for his tribe.

## Town Crier News

- Brant's Indian name was *Thayendanegea,* which means "he places two bets."

- Brant was educated by **missionaries.** He was a religious leader among his people as well as a warrior.

*Joseph Brant posed for this portrait in London, England, in 1776.*

# From Revolution to Independence

**The actions of a group of discontented colonists changed history. After the Revolutionary War, the North American colonies became an independent nation.**

The Revolutionary War was won not only by soldiers and officers on the battlefield, but by the many **statesmen,** writers, merchants, craftsmen, **camp followers,** slaves, and Native Americans who fought for independence in whatever way they could. Men, women, and children throughout the colonies worked together to reach a common goal of freedom from British rule. They set strong examples of patriotism, bravery, and cooperation for us to follow today. Their determination and spirit led to the creation of a new nation.

*The people cheered as George Washington returned to New York City on November 25, 1783. The war for independence was over at last, and British troops were leaving the colonies.*

# Glossary

**apprentice**   person who works for a skilled tradesperson or craftsperson to learn a trade or skill

**camp follower**   woman who traveled with army troops doing tasks for the soldiers such as laundry, mending clothes, cooking, and nursing the wounded. Many of these women were wives of the soldiers.

**colony**   territory settled by people from other countries who still had loyalty to those other countries. The word *colonist* is used to describe a person who lives in a colony. The word *colonial* is used to describe things related to a colony.

**commission**   official paper that gives a person military rank and authority; often bought by wealthy people who wanted to make the military their career

**Continental Congress**   group of representatives from the colonies who carried out the duties of the government

**discharge**   to relieve someone from his or her duties; specifically, to remove someone from military service

**discontent**   feeling of not being happy with something

**document**   legal or official paper

**engraver**   person who carves designs onto a material such as glass or metal

**fife**   small flute

**French and Indian War**   called the Seven Years' War in Europe. From 1754 to 1763, Britain fought against France in the North American colonies. Some Native Americans—called Indians at the time—helped the French.

**indentured servant**   person who agreed to work for another person for a set period of time to repay a debt

**inherit**   to receive the money or property of a person who has died

**legislature**   group of people with the power to make laws

**Loyalist**   colonist who supported the British government during the American Revolution

**major general**   officer ranked one level above a general

**militia**   group of ordinary men who fought to protect the colonies before the Revolutionary War, and then fought alongside the Continental Army during the war. Men who fought in a militia were called *militiamen*.

**missionary**   person who tries to get others to follow a specific religion

**negotiate**   to try to come to an agreement between two or more people or groups

**outpost**   small military fort

**Parliament**   lawmakers of the British government

**Patriot**   person during colonial times who believed that the colonies should break away from the rule of Great Britain and form their own government

**private**   soldier of the lowest military ranking

**rebellion**   act of trying to overthrow a legal government

**resign**   to volunteer to give up a position or job

**statesman**   person who carries out public or government business

**traitor**   person who turns against the country to which he or she was once loyal

**viceroy**   person who was appointed by the ruler of a country to govern another colony or country that belonged to that ruler

**West Point**   site in the Hudson River Valley; location of George Washington's headquarters in 1779; command post Benedict Arnold attempted to betray to the British in 1780; after 1802, the site of a U.S. military academy

# Historical Fiction to Read

Banim, Lisa. *A Spy in the King's Colony.* New York: Silver Moon Press, 1998.
Eleven-year-old Emily Parker is living in Boston in 1775. She is a Patriot, and she suspects
her neighbor Robert of being a Loyalist spy.

Denenberg, Barry. *The Journal of William Thomas Emerson: A Revolutionary War Patriot,
Boston, Massachusetts, 1774.* New York: Scholastic, 1998.
A twelve-year-old orphan boy keeps a diary of his experiences before and during the
Revolutionary War.

Gregory, Kristiana. *The Winter of Red Snow: The Revolutionary War Diary of Abigail Jane Stewart,
Valley Forge, Pennsylvania, 1777.* New York: Scholastic, 1996.
A young girl living close to the military camp at Valley Forge writes in her diary about the
things she sees.

Schurfranz, Vivian. *A Message for General Washington.* New York: Silver Moon Press, 1998.
A twelve-year-old girl travels from her home in Yorktown, Virginia, to bring an important
message to General George Washington.

# Historical Places to Visit

**Boston National Historical Park**
Charlestown Navy Yard
Boston, Massachusetts 02129-4543
Visitor Information: (617) 242-5642
Take the Freedom Trail walking tour of the park to see sixteen Revolutionary War sites and
structures. Visit downtown Boston to see the Old State House and the Paul Revere House.
Visit Charlestown to see the Bunker Hill Monument.

**Independence National Historical Park**
313 Walnut Street
Philadelphia, Pennsylvania 19106
Visitor Information: (215) 597-8974
Visit the place where the Declaration of Independence and the U.S. Constitution were written
and signed. Tour downtown Philadelphia to see the Liberty Bell, Independence Hall, and
other historical landmarks of the Revolutionary War.

**Minute Man National Historical Park**
174 Liberty Street
Concord, Massachusetts 01742
Visitor Information: (978) 369-6993
This park stretches across the historic sites of some of the opening battles of the
Revolutionary War. Visit the sites of the battles at Concord, Lincoln, and Lexington.

# Index